# Extranjera

# Extranjera

Poems

## Lola Haskins

Story Line Press | *Pasadena, CA*

ISBN 978-1-58654-060-9 (tradepaper)
978-1-58654-092-0 (casebound)

The National Endowment for the Arts, the Los Angeles County Arts Commission, the Ahmanson Foundation, the Dwight Stuart Youth Fund, the Max Factor Family Foundation, the Pasadena Tournament of Roses Foundation, the Pasadena Arts & Culture Commission and the City of Pasadena Cultural Affairs Division, the City of Los Angeles Department of Cultural Affairs, the Audrey & Sydney Irmas Charitable Foundation, the Kinder Morgan Foundation, the Meta & George Rosenberg Foundation, the Allergan Foundation, the Riordan Foundation, Amazon Literary Partnership, and the Mara W. Breech Foundation partially support Red Hen Press.

Second Edition
Published by Story Line Press
an imprint of Red Hen Press
www.redhen.org

## Acknowledgments

The author wishes to acknowledge and thank the editors of the following periodicals in whose pages the following poems first appeared: *Americas Review, Artful Dodge, Boulevard, Caprice, Crazyhorse, Free Lunch, International Quarterly, Kalliope, Kestrel, London Magazine, London Review of Books, Missouri Review, Ploughshares, Tampa Review.*

# Contents

## 3

## 4

## México

I have lived here before but always
I have retreated. It is afraid
staying in a language where you
were not born.  Where vowels seem
soft but throb mercilessly on
like this bruja sun which will not
die, but burns into the night.

I have looked in this mirror
and looked down. I have sung
canciones to make me weep
and denied the tears. I have
never owned those receptacles
which hold hearts. It is afraid.

I have said no to the flies in me.
I have refused to tongue the red
and juicy seeds heaped in cups.
But this time, though I climb faintly
up the bus's purring stairs,
though at first it is afraid to see,
this time I say Yes.  Yes I am
willing now.  Yes foreign is a word
for fear. Yes I am coming home.

1

## Eclipse

The government says women
will not birth monsters,
that pigs will still nurse their young,
that corn will not shrink to ash.
But who believes the government?

It is noon and night is falling.
You and I look only down.
We are afraid of what might be
glowing in the air.
We know that there are

some truths so terrible
that to face them
would whiten our eyes forever.

## Wait for Us

Watchful boys, gleams in their pockets,
circle the plaza where a television
explains El Gran Eclipse de México
as though the moon crossing the sun
belongs to this nation whose anthem
shouts of war.
               This is Uruápan.
You can walk under the palms in
the Parque Nacional, where banyans
cast complicated roots, and bananas
hang in thick fingers. You can hear
the shouts of children practicing
insults and fighting, the many uses
of teeth.
              But now it is night
and the foreigner is at risk.
The soft white foreigner. We walk
fast. They begin to follow us.
They quicken. *Espéranos*, they call.

## The Pyramids at Tsuntsinsan

Tried to rise, like an old man
in a deep chair, but collapsed
into themselves, not all at once
but by the weather slowly,
the way a son who will soon
leave home, stays out more and
more.
   Tiny signs, half-gone in
green, brought us here.  We
climbed angry, through the rank
smells of flower and snake.
We struggled for footing on
the scattered hill. We argued.
Til the pyramids struck us dumb.

## Monday Morning in la Plaza de las Armas

Tiny plastic soldiers dangle from
their parachutes. They litter
the power lines and the higher
branches of trees. Red and blue and
yellow shreds punctuate the scene.
The air is grey. It is very still.

Not like yesterday when the Plaza
teemed with Papí! Mamí! Por favor!
And vendors handed over the little
men, and balloons, and dulces spiny
with coconut. Then BANG and BANG
as small fists clutched what were
not any more balloons. And soldiers
which Paco or Ana or Luis had thought
to take home and keep forever sailed
out of reach and no Papí, however
rich, could bring them back again.

The soldiers rock a little as a wind
comes up, rock softly, like lullabies.

## Street Level

He brandishes a fan of fly swatters,
yellow and blue and green.
*Para las moscas*, he sings
and *barrato barrato* like the buzzing
of flies.  He is perhaps five.
Later, he will build castles with his sister
from tar that has been heaped in the street.
His dark brown hands will turn black.
The light will fail.  Molding the tar in
battlements, he will be completely happy.

# Three Views from the Latin American Summit

*Guadalajara, Jalisco 1994*

*i*

Important men hold forth to an ocean
of campesinos with armbands and banners.
Slogans fly like spray.  On the edges
of the crowd, shoeshine boys quote
prices.  After, they say they meant
per shoe.  And foreigners pay,
their faces red for their poor Spanish.

*ii*

She leans slack to the wall.
Bright flies cluster where
her eyes ooze. A visitor in
a grey suit, his belly ripe as
a fat papaya, breaks his stride.
She palms the coins.
Her hand is empty. Her hand
has always been empty.

*iii*

In the Plaza del Catedrál they have
sandblasted the nudes, which shine
fresh green, their instruments
in their arms. The unswept sand
crunches underfoot. At any moment
a wave may break, here over this city,
hundreds of miles from the coast.

## Roofs

Of banged-on tin that never shone.
Twisted scrap-tin full of holes so
light dots the dirt floor inside.


Of red tiles cured in sun, lapping
over like a dance, the way a husband
curves over his wife's cupped body.

Of banana leaves, wing on wing.
A child lies inside, wasted by
the sick water. His eyes are flame.

## Salvation in a Catholic Country

As we enter, Gabriel palms
our key.  He slides it
across the slick desk.
He knows our number.
He knows where we will go
from here, the elevators
by which we will rise.
He knows the doors
that will open by themselves.

In La Concordia, life
is simple:  the smell of
*arepas* ascending the air
shaft, the chitter of maids
watching the soaps in
the next room, the heavy
cleansing rains that stop
before we can even count
our sins. This is thin air.
Climbing these hills,
how easily we leave
breath behind.

## Los Viejitos

They leer from market stalls,
lean crudely carved in their
hundreds, on sticks of canes.
In the better hotels, you can
see them dance.  First, though,
their conjunto squeaks a set,
its violins so out of tune a dog
would run.  And then at last
the old men, bent double,
enter in a twist. They pause.
They stomp their canes.
They exhibit, one by one.
Finally, in a burst of claps
they clog off-stage. When
they lift their masks, we glimpse
that even these are children.
They will overwhelm us all.

2

## Sobre Transportes del Norte

He leans across the aisle and points
out my window to a field where three
streams of water gush straight up.
*Agua caliente,* he says. *De la tierra.*
We are nearing Zamora. The bus
slides by the blue wall of the plastics
factory. PRD says the wall. And
PRI. All México is coming to a boil.

*Yo soy de Salinas*, he says. *California.*
He pulls his wallet out of his jeans,
scratches his undershirted stomach,
and passes me three folded sheets.
*See?* He says. *Tickets.* They are damp
from riding under him. *Drunk driving,*
he says, proudly. *One more and they
put me in jail. I like cerveza too much.*
And he grins, and his teeth are so white
I think they would glow in the dark.

He folds the papers, leans back, puts
them away again. We are passing
fields of maguey, full of broken glass
that glitters in the sun. I am foreign.
There is so much I do not understand.

## Catedral

Below the gold Virgin, notes fade.
*My son in California would die*
*but I prayed to you.  Bless you*
*that Tía Ángela is safe.*
                              Besides
the notes, four wordless snapshots
from a photo booth. Young boys.
Under each is taped a car key.
*Protect them, Holy Mother, where*
*they go.*
              On her knees, an old woman
is crossing the stone. Her rebozo
trails its fringe of black and blue.
When she reaches the altar rail,
she opens her palms.
She feels them fill with light.

## Nopales

They start before dawn, baskets airy on their heads,
two old sisters, climbing the rock-strewn hill.
In the forest of cacti, they turn small, reaching
up to slice the thick leaves from their stems.
Already, Rosa's thumb is festering. She scrapes
at it with her knife. The sharp spines break,
burrow deeper. She wonders where her children
sleep, gone these years across the border.
Wading at night. Running away from her to L.A.,
as far away as the stars.
                         When Teresita starts
for home, Rosa follows. They heft the baskets
from their backs. The chickens squawk and scatter.
Teresita squats, fans the coals to flame.
                         Rosa
feels a flush, like that of a young girl, spread
across her face. *La Virgen*. Walking towards
them in her blue rebozo. The light beginning
over the hills is the light of miracles.

## El Milagro

Adela sees the pig ascend to heaven.
One moment, he's rooting in the muddy
street. The next he's in a golden cloud,
rising above the red tile roofs.
He swirls and vanishes. *Alleluia*
Adela hears from the catedral and all
the bells start ringing. Surely this
was some holy pig, to be taken to live
among God and all His angels. Perhaps
he was never a pig at all. Adela
makes the sign of the cross. As her
shaking fingers calm, Adela knows
she will never again eat pork.

## Her Story

Her palms pale with masa.
The tortillas on her drum are freckled moons.
Black braids lie down her back.  Her apron

is fading the way dusk
blurs the edges of the island so its shrine
turns to air.  When the bus plunged off

the twisting road
like a bird folded sharp, and her brother's flesh
charred to meat, she did not care about God

or the flaming wreck
that called itself Three Stars of Gold.
She lives alone now, speaks to no one but

the fish in the lake
that rise to the scraps she throws, then
vanish into the twilit water like prayer.

## The Fish they call Sierra

### i

They name it for how it leaps, for its wish
to become sky.

They name it for the high air between the peaks
of its tail.

They name it for what they crave, mountains thick
as fish, swimming in their thousands towards
the horizon forever.

### ii

The cheeks of Tarascan men are smooth
as the sheened red clay that their women
shape to birds, from whose mouths
water pours.
                    Mornings, the men launch
their boats. They cast nets into the fog.
When the nets begin to move
in their hands, they lean into what they
cannot see, and pull, until the fog itself
turns silver.
                    And they go on pulling until
they are up to their knees in fish, until
there is no place on the bottom of the boat
which does not move.

*iii*

Rosalia slits the last sierra
and removes its curled insides.
She dips her knife into the lake.
The pulse at her wrist turns
cool. On her hip the baby stirs,
unclenches the star of his hand.

## La Estrella

*The star is everywhere,* says Miguel.
*Today I saw it on a wall.*

*It is on the forehead of the Virgin,*
says Mamá, and *it is outside too,*

*in the dark, higher than the arches*
*of the catedral. And also here,*

says Miguel, opening his fist.
*This one fell down one day.*

*I caught it on its way to the sea.*
*And mira, Mamá, all those.* And

they lean their heads out the window
where there is no glass,

out into the night where mariachis
of stars are glittering,

hard and bright as jewels on a shoe.
Miguel looks down at his bare toes.

His mother picks him up. His hand
is closed, holding his star safe.

## Caballos

The painted horses of the carneval
have been covered for the night.  Under
that black cloth they gallop still,
hard around the mirrored dark, circling
the small gold lights to the organ's
wheezy tune, and always on their backs,
the warm hands of niños, their chubby legs
gripping as if the caballos were going
somewhere wild, beyond the earshot
of criadas, gossiping in the back patio,
to places their parents  can never know
who think their children safe in bed
when they've kissed their drowsy
cheeks goodnight, and shut the door.

## Peluquero

On the street, a man is losing his hair.
He slumps, head bent, neck exposed.
Across the man's shoulders, stuck to
a grubby towel, blue-black clippings
strew, and around the man's huaraches,
wetly on his bare toes, the thick hairs
rain.
     So easily could he die, and by
this grafittied wall and on such a day
as this, in spring, having sat down
harmless, thinking nothing

                     as around
the corner a sudden camión comes
blasting, and the peluquero leaps
away, lurches into the man's chair,
bright scissors in his forward hand.

## Cuando Morimos

Hernán fell. He used not to be afraid
climbing scaffolds, his hammer banging
at his hip the way a woodpecker bangs a tree.
Used never to fear walking that high slant,
his mouth studded with nails.

Now we carry his box through the streets,
the box in which he lies, his hat in his hands.
It is a long way out of town and dust coats us
all. We have put on masks, birds and jaguars,
the faces of moths. Hernán's is the only true
face. And Hernán fell.

The building rises which Hernán built.
El Palacio del Gobierno, it will be, where
el señor presidente municipal will sit, the
new palacio whose roof is strong, whose
air is full of falling. And we will all of us
do business in its rooms.

## Nombres

We name our streets for desire. *Calzada de la Independencia* rotates through the destinations of buses which bulge like heavy bellies, which pass the rooftops lined with police, bristling with assault rifles. There is an election. PRI says God and the ballots of the dead.

We name our children for God. Jesús for the glowing heart and blessing hand. Jesús for the peace we crave, carrying warm tortillas home. María for the Virgen. And we wear tight skirts and blouses which curve to make a man's hand itch as we dream of streets lined with brides, white as first communions. Then we pass through those windows, and on the other side . . . How dark it is. How we cannot breathe.

We name our holidays for the dead. We eat buñuelos iced with skulls and we play with tiny skeletons, jointed and dancing. We feast for our dead mothers and uncles. We breathe the fragrant steam and let the tamales alone. We drink cerveza into the candled night and celebrate that life is short.

## Lengthening Light

*Y ser como ese sol, que lento expira,*
*algo muy luminoso que se pierde.*
                              *—Miguel Nájera*


My shadow over the plaza is growing long.
The stalls of bracelets are gleaming,
lapis lazuli like half-shut eyes.
My skin in the late day is darkening.

The shade is slow leaves, slowly fading.
Soon it will be lost for the sun will leave it
like a faithless lover over and over
gets up and goes away until all shade is

one shadow over the plaza and why have I
come?  It is afraid, staying in a language
where I was not born.  Yet I am learning
words for a voice known in any tongue

as the certainty of night arrives and I
await the stars with such fear I cannot
tell you.  Have you noticed old women,
their arms circled in lapis, a ring

on every wrinkled finger?  I take a table,
ask for café con leche.  I sip it
slowly, making it last.  I am admiring
the beautiful lengthening light.

3

## The Man in the Large and Glittering Hat

Thinks the star flurried down
and settled on his head.


He walks between the rickety
tables his guitar poised


looking into the women's eyes.
Hesitation is enough. He is


singing of kisses. Natalia imagines
him lifting her hair, to reveal


the place no larger than a centavo
behind her ear. She imagines


the damp of his lips. He's a bobo,
she thinks.  In her dream his hands


are all over her. She looks up, sees
the hat, like a galaxy, on its peg.

## El Café

Stone arches frame the table where the man has joined Melinda. She does not know him. They order coffee. He sets his briefcase down, rests one hand on the table. The hand is a furred spider, the kind that lives under wood. Once there was a hurricane off the coast, such blowing rain, such wind, that the avocados the lined the hills were blasted from their roots. After, she went with Papá to see. He rolled a downed branch with his foot and from it there crawled such a spider.

The coffee comes in tiny cups. She adds sugar. He taps a long ash from his cigarette and Melinda, who has never smoked, is seized with the desire to begin. The man pulls charts from his briefcase, lays them on the table. "Here" he says, and "There", touching the numbers as if they were cities. Melinda says "Yes" and "Oh, I see" and her breath is growing short. She licks the foam from the creamy edge of her cup.

A boy, bent under a load of straw masks, pauses at their table. Melinda buys one, puts it on. She leaves with the man. In his room there is an altar, a Virgin surrounded with flowers. He makes love to Melinda's woven face. Later, she goes home. Her husband asks her about the coffee in that café. Is it still black and strong, a bullet in the throat? Did she enjoy lingering? Melinda shows him the mask.

## *Ja Ja*

The guard at the jewelry store sights along the barrel of his
rifle.  He follows the pretty girl, keeping her chest in the center
of his cross-hairs.  She sees him from the corner of her eye.  She
hurries. The tiny heart on her ankle chain tinkles busily.
She rounds the corner, he lowers the gun. *Ja, ja.*

## El Mercado

In the center of the mercado,
the dark and crowded aisles open to the sky.
Here Alicia stands one early morning
when all the stalls are covered and tied,
as by families moving far away.  And
she rubs the bruises with her thumb,
deliberately in one direction as
one would rub silver to raise
a shine.

And Alicia thinks this dawn is
home, not Miguel, with the black crescents
under his nails, and the creases in his
knuckles black.  Who pressed hard against her,
flattening her breasts. Not Miguel,
with his mouthful of rage, ready to
spit it on her and, when she moved
back, ready to show what he
could do.

The first rays of sun streak
the plaza. Everywhere, the covers are
coming off.  There are shoes and
belts and saddles for sale. There is
rope.  No one was leaving after all.

## The Carver of Masks

He works the knife.
   The shavings fall curled
with the faint scent of burns.
     He is making slits.
Through such slits one can hardly see.  One is
forever eight,
   peering through cracks at Mamá's
screams
  until his mouth is stopped
     by Papá's borracho
hand.
  The mouth's a gash, a slash of blood surprise.
He works faster, cuts the suggestion of a nose, two
holes like a snout.
   *Pig*, he thinks, and wipes his knife
on his jeans.

## The Platanillos

Mira, says the child, pointing.
*The platanillos are bleeding.*


*You are only little*, says her mother,
looking up from the river


where she is washing small underpants
against the rocks. *Bring me that soap.*


The child fetches the thick bar.  She
looks up.  The sky is darkening.


Jaime went to live with God.  Red
leaked from his eyes and ears.


Jaime was even littler than she is.
They light candles for him every mass


but sometimes, the candles go out.
Maybe Jaime is angry.  The sky


turns black. There is a smell of
burnt wick.  It begins to rain.


*Mamá!* calls the child. *Mamá!*
Her mother goes on with her work.

The child scrambles up the bank. When
she brushes against the platanillos,


blood comes off on her hands.

## Ligia

The family sleeps. Their hammocks
sway gently, like boats on air.
The casa fills with their slow
breathing.
　　　　　There is a black swan
painted on a plate. Ligia pumps
water over her. The swan shakes
glaze from her feet.
　　　　　　　　Ligia leans
dreaming, elbows propped on the
splintered windowsill. The swan
has settled on the dim lake, just out
from shore. She floats there,
so beautiful. The moon
silvers the mesh of Antonio's nets
between the house and the swan,
where he has spread them to dry.

*Straw*

A man's sombrero with its one
tiny tassel.

A woman's broom, to gather
what has fallen
and return it to the air.

Swans and tied stars
hung in strings.

What the child, rocking in his
hammock dreams:

That the light he sees is made
of grass.

That the most beautiful pájaros
are grass also

and he hears their far calls,
like wheat, whispering
in a field.

## Angel del Temblor

Fallen bronze head, your welds apart,
your huge and gentle body broken
as Teresa, robozoed in the garden
of the museum.  Teresa lurching,
fallen as an angel after the quake,
the last to be made whole.

Teresa likes tequila best because
it tells her she can go home, up
the muddy mountain road to La Piedad,
that her sisters will be there still,
little than she, and she can cradle
Angelita, new and small, and sing
to her until she sleeps.  But always
the song ends, in a cardboard box
draped with plastic in the city
where the eagle talons the snake
and you have to steal to live.
                                        Oh, but
angel, heavier than a man can lift,
help this woman who sinks
to the bench, so sad and dark.
Show her how even in the deepest
temblor,  something will be saved.

A shaft of shine angles from the clouds
polishing the angel's parts :  robe, hands
hair, and still intact, the wings.
                                        Teresa gets up,
passes through the museum gate, out
into the street. The bougainvilla
are all in pink. It is such a pretty day,
and though she is the oldest, Teresa
almost skips.  She is so happy, just
holding Angelita's hand.

## Juan of the Angels

Sits inside the darkened bar. The hotel
no longer pays him for the songs
his fingers make on the instrument
which is the marriage of his hands.
Instead, they bring him coca or cidral.
And when the bar's shadow spills
outside, and the stars come out,
they bring him beer.

                    Every day Juan
leans more deeply on his cane but
still he comes. Guests buy him drinks.
Sometimes they stop talking. Juan
plays on, talk or none. All his melodies
are hungers.

                  One evening a boy,
perhaps fourteen, comes in.
The boy says nothing, listens with
his eyes. Juan cradles his guitar.
*Soy gitano*, he says. Gypsy.
The boy, who speaks no Spanish
thinks Juan is saying his name,
so he says *Django*, and points to
his own thin chest. Juan offers
him the guitar, with its mouth
of mother of pearl and the small
moons along the frets.

                      The boy
bends over. His dark hair falls
over his face. He makes the song
young Juan would play for the women
to dance. All night the same strum.
The women's skirts swirl around
the long fires. The stars are
turning pale.

                The boy plays on alone.

## Waiting for the Bus

She casts the only shade at the crossroad.
She has set the huge basket down
full of sticks to sell,
which she slings with her rebozo over
her shoulder.
          Her bare feet feel the dust
no more than stones do, but there is beginning
in her head
        a sort of flying.
               She counts
the ribs of a cow shifting under its stretched
skin, as it mouths the sparse grass between
the rocks.
         She sings to herself a song with
her name
    *Si Adelita se fuera con otro, la seguiría*
*por tierra y por mar*
            But the heat is a dry sea
and a wind is coming up, and she is feeling
what she felt when she first saw the young
soldier in his glorious uniform, her Juan
who died this morning,
          his few coins arranged
in the dirt by the bruja to stop the pain,
la bruja who took the coins and went away.
And somehow
     Adela's smooth braids are turning
to wings, and the road is spinning, and *Ay,*
she thinks, soaring above the desert, free
in the hard blue sky.
         *He is seeking me by air.*

*The Liberator*

She is five years old, wearing pink ruffles and shiny black shoes, and socks white as candles. Mamá is taking her to see the murals. Mamá tells her how Hidalgo's army set fire to the Alhóndiga, how they burst in and killed everyone inside. Even the women, Mamá says. She tells her how, since Hidalgo was a priest and his cause was just, the Virgin of Guadaloupe watched over him that day. It was a great victory, Mamá says. For freedom. They are walking into a patio. She looks up and sees Hidalgo there, painted huge across the arches. The padre's hands are open. But it is his eyes that catch the orange flames around him, his eyes that cover her body with burns.

She is twenty. She wears jeans to class. She leaves nervous red rings around her cigarettes. She has learned how to dance, pressed to the small movements of Guillermo's hips. Yet sometimes the cross on Mamá's bedroom wall seems to glow, and she feels an edge to her fingers, as if they do not know quite what to do. And some nights, the clothes on her chair seem to take shape. And rise. And they are taller than all her dreams and the shadows they cast are tinged with orange, like the light under the door of a burning room. And sometimes she thinks her own life, her breasts, her legs, her deep black hair, is a prison and that she will never escape.

## La Señora de García-Marcos Considers

Can I cover me with a snake?
Shall I span my mouth with colored wings?
How I have longed for a wooden face
that will not melt.

His slaps will leave no marks on me.
If his kisses wear me thin, I can
paint me back.  I will show a smile
as beautiful as a rock.  I will

wear the hat of some high office.
If I enter a room, gasps will follow.
I will talk freely then, flashing
my jeweled wrists and hands.

4

## Uchepas

Tamales plain-steamed then whitened
like a wedding dress with cream
and queso. A beautiful, simple food.
But not enough. We want more.

We are cravers of storms and choques
on the highway. We never mind
waiting in the long stopped lines
if at the end, there can be some blood.

Forget our lovers. We want a stranger,
shiver deepest at the hairs on the
backs of someone's hands, who
has not touched us, yet.

## Guayabas

Puckered pears
arranged in hard pyramids on the stone.
Beneath green rind, white flesh.
The curve of the guayaba
the curve of my palm.

An Indian woman,
not young, heavy in her striped shirt.
Her long braids, deeper than starlings'
wings.  In the slowly falling light,
the curve of her cheek.

## The Meaning of Taquitos

She flips bits of meat into small limp
tortillas, arranges them in petals on
a heavy green plate, splashed with swans.
I choose one, drown it in salsa. When she
looks away, I look down, into the pot
at the simmering head  its horns gone
its eyes out  its flesh shredded. Only
the jawbone does not yield, the jaw
with its flat teeth sunken, like
an instrument a squatting man might
play.

    *He grips the jaw between his knees,*
*drums with bones sheened opium by*
*the moon. And his voice is a low howl*
*and his hands. . . . his hands are*
*quickening.*

               How long has this Indio
been standing beside me, salsa dripping
between his fingers, his mouth rimmed
red? A few moments. Thousands of years.

## In the Market, Jesús Cleans Fish

One slick hand slides in,
comes up jeweled.  Red ropes,
slithers of veiny pink,
fall to his brimming tub.

The other holds the fish.
So silver is this fish.
The air inside it breathes
like Lupe sleeping.  He

strokes its slippery flesh,
rolls it between his fingers.
No. Not like Lupe sleeping.
Like Lupe when she moans.

## Dog

The dog on the roof leans snarling.
His ribs grin from his sides.
His lips peel back like fruit.
His gums are pale blood, and wet.

The street is littered with mango
skins and feces.  Dirty water
runs along the stone.  The stucco
is falling from the houses.

The dog on the roof leans snarling.
The hairs rise on my arms.
I want the dog.

## Casa

I am walled and on my walls
are glass teeth.
Sharp jewels of green and amber.
Clear shards to catch the light
the way a bride turns her ring.

Inside, soft red flowers open.
Inside, yellow bougainvilla glitters
like the yellow specks in my eyes.
Oh, if you would be a thief
come crawling.  Come bleeding.
Come to me in ribbons.

## Blood

In the market, a bull's head.
Horned still, with black lips.
A boy is carving from the cheek,
slides the slices off his palm.
Green flies gather on the cuts
like jewels.
      In the disco-bar,
Amalia, in her thin black
dress. Rafael, who is gone,
used to hurt her.  A perfume
drifts from Amalia's skin.
Men buzz, oil their hair,
hurry across the room.

## El Grito de Dolores

A bus passes.
I drink its sweet, black air.
The bus jumped the curb, cornering.
The bus slammed through the potholes.
I want to do that too.
With my rear view mirror hung with saints.
With my radio blaring *Guadalajara*.
As if it were always night, and I drunk.
Banging through the unlit streets,
past the bars with their half doors,
past the tequila factory
past Tlaquepaque. Rattling fast
in the wrong lane. You, Martín
with your macho fists. You with your
wet lips. Get off the road.

## Chiles: A Birthday Poem

Lanterns, orange and veined
Hot red birds
Green fires

Long dry withered maroons
with seeds that rattle
like old men full of passion . . .

You in the front row, whispering
to your companion wearing pearls,
I no longer care what you think.
I will be who I am.

# Final

*Me moriré in Paris, con aguacero.*
          *—Cesar Vallejo*

*I will die in Tonalá among the ceramic hamburgers.*
*I think I will have in my hand some very small*
*souvenirs-- a duck, a doll's olla, a tiny snake.*
*And these will be like what I have tried to make*
*with grains of words, fired hard. Something for*
*your child. And the duck will not have real wings*
*but painted ones, done by the eyelashes*
*of dreams. And the olla will hold a comida*
*whose sweetness you can hardly imagine because*
*you cannot smell so small. And the snake*
*will be a good snake. When I am gone, it can*
*live in your heart.*
          *And it will be the weather*
*of my abuela, whose hair brooked no white,*
*her México of hard skies blue as the rim*
*of a glass. And I will not fall. I will simply*
*sit down, by a little girl in ragged pink*
*and her friend with the dusty knees, who*
*are playing a game among some boxes because*
*at that moment, more than I have ever wanted*
*anything in my life, I will want to play too.*

# Spanish Glossary and Notes

*abuela*; grandmother

*agua caliente*: literally "hot water", refers to a hot spring which is gushing high into the air

*arepas*: a food of central Mexico, made from masa harina (corn flour) and filled with various meats

*barrato*: cheap

*bobo*: clown, idiot

*bruja*: witch

*buñuelos*: sweet rolls

*caballo*: horse

*camión*: city bus

*canciones*: songs

*cerveza*: beer

*choques*: accidents (car wrecks)

*coca* : Coca Cola

*cidral*: an apple-flavored soft drink

*conjunto*: a musical group

*cuando morimos*: when we die

*Django*: Django Reinhart, a famous French jazz guitarist.

*dulces*: sweets

*El Grito de Dolores*: the rallying cry for the Mexican war of independence from Spain in the early nineteenth century. Lola is a nickname for Dolores.

*espéranos*: wait for us

*estrella*: star

*Guadalajara*: a typical mariachi song about the capital of Jalisco

*guayaba*: a green fruit

*ja ja*: Ha ha

*la Virgen*: the virgin, ie Mary

*Los Viejitos*: literally "Little Old Men", a dance from Michoacán made up by Indians to mock the Spanish *maguey*: the cactus from which tequila is made

*mariachi*: a band which plays traditional folk music, identified
        especially with Jalisco

*masa (harina)*: the corn flour from which tortillas are made

*mercado*: market

*milagro*: miracle

*nombres*: names

*nopales*: the fleshy leaves of the prickly pear, eaten as a vegetable

*olla*: a clay cooking pot

*pájaros*: birds

*Palacio del Gobierno*: City Hall

*para las moscas*: for the flies

*peluquero*: barber

*platanillo*: a large red iris-like flower which grows in damp places

PRI and PRD: political parties

*presidente municipal*: mayor

*queso*: cheese

*rebozo*: shawl

*Si Adelita se fuera con otro, la seguiría por tierra y por mar*: a
        line from "Adelita" a traditional love song: If Adelita
        were to go off with someone else, I would follow her by
        land and by sea

*sierra*: literally "mountain range," the name of a fish caught in
        Pátzcuaro's lake

*Transportes del Norte*: the name of a bus company

*temblor*: earthquake

*"the eagle talons the snake"*: refers to the legend, in which the
        founders of Mexico City were shown where to build by
        an eagle with a snake in its claws

*Tres Estrellas de Oro*: Three Stars of Gold: another bus company

*uchepas*: breakfast tamales typical of Michoacán

*yo soy de Salinas*: I'm from Salinas

## Biographical Note

Lola Haskins has published twelve books of poetry and three of prose. Her work has appeared in the *Atlantic, Hudson Review, Georgia Review, Southern Review, Prairie Schooner, London Review of Books*, and elsewhere, as well as having been broadcast on BBC and NPR. Among her honors are the Iowa Poetry Prize, two Florida Book Awards, two National Endowment for the Arts fellowships, and the Emily Dickinson Prize from Poetry Society of America. She currently serves as Honorary Chancellor of the Florida State Poets Association.